THE ROOKIE HANDBOOK

A QUICK REFERENCE GUIDE TO CALLS FORSERVICE.

Xavier Wells

Copyright 2018 by Xavier Wells

All rights reserved.

ISBN 9781983398537

Table of Contents

Preface   v
Advice   vii
Terminology   ix

NON-VIOLENT CALLS FOR SERVICE   1

Chapter One	Alarm Calls	3
Chapter Two	Animal Calls	7
Chapter Three	Auto Theft Calls	11
Chapter Four	Burglary Calls	14
Chapter Five	Crash Calls	19
Chapter Six	Criminal Trespass Calls	27
Chapter Seven	Disturbance Calls	29
Chapter Eight	Drug Calls	35
Chapter Nine	Fire Calls	37
Chapter Ten	Flooding/Natural Disaster Calls	40
Chapter Eleven	Forgery/Id Crime Calls	42
Chapter Twelve	Found Property Calls	43
Chapter Thirteen	Hang Up Calls	45
Chapter Fourteen	Missing Person Calls	47
Chapter Fifteen	Noise Complaint Calls	49
Chapter Sixteen	Parking Calls	51
Chapter Seventeen	Pedestrian in Roadway/ Traffic Hazard Calls	53

Chapter Eighteen	Public Intoxication Calls	55
Chapter Nineteen	Stranded Motorist Calls	57
Chapter Twenty	Suspicious Calls	59
Chapter Twenty-One	Theft Calls	63
Chapter Twenty-Two	Welfare Check Calls	66

VIOLENT CALLS **69**

Chapter Twenty-Three	Abuse Calls	71
Chapter Twenty-Four	Assault Calls	74
Chapter Twenty-Five	Bomb Calls	77
Chapter Twenty-Six	Death/Murder Calls	79
Chapter Twenty-Seven	Family Violence Calls	81
Chapter Twenty-Eight	Hit and Run Calls	83
Chapter Twenty-Nine	Robbery Calls	85
Chapter Thirty	Sexual Assault Calls	89

Author's Ending Remarks   93

Preface

The worst feeling as a rookie is when someone on scene calls you a rookie. It zaps the thunder out of your commands and takes away from your police presence. Educating yourself is the only real way to ensure your confidence on the street. Sadly, there aren't nearly enough resources available out there to help new rookies succeed.

This book is by no means meant to replace the years of experience on the streets; that can only be gained on the job. However, this book can and will give you an on-hand resource and study guide to help you make confident decisions in critical as well as everyday situations in the field of law enforcement. This book is a comprehensive guide to the best practices for practically every call one could face in the field of law enforcement. It is meant to keep you focused on what the end outcome should look like, regardless of how hectic the scene may be.

Advice

- Never run the victim!
- Slow everything down once the scene is secure.
- Always check the shoes and socks.

Terminology

Secure the Scene—ultimately this means show up and make sure you know what you are dealing with, look for any potential ambushes, and then establish you police presence.

Run—criminal history and involvement check on a person.

DOB—Date of Birth

CSI—Crime Scene Investigation

NON-VIOLENT CALLS FOR SERVICE

Chapter One

ALARM CALLS

Alarm Call/No Sign of Forced Entry
Officer Safety Considerations:

- Park 2–3 houses/buildings down from your target location.
- As you approach keep an eye out for obvious signs of forced entry or occupation.
- Have service weapon at the ready.
- Secure the scene.

Objectives/Outcomes:

- Upon approach, cover and clear as much of the structure's perimeter as possible, looking out for broken windows, busted doors, or anything out of the ordinary.
- If no signs of forced entry are found, try the locks on the doors of the house/business to ensure the structure is secure.

- If all entryways are locked and secure, knock and announce your presence as a law enforcement officer.
- If someone answers the door, verify their right to be at the location and document their identification.
- If no one answers, consider the structure secure and clear the scene.

Alarm Call/Signs of Forced Entry

Officer Safety Considerations:

- Park 2–3 houses/buildings down from your target location.
- As you approach, keep an eye out for obvious signs of forced entry or occupation.
- Have service weapon at the ready.
- Secure the scene.

Objectives/Outcomes:

- Upon approach, cover and clear as much of the structure's perimeter as possible, looking out for broken windows, busted doors, or anything out of the ordinary.
- When a sign of forced entry is found, notify dispatch over the radio, request backup, and keep a visual on as many of the structure's exits as possible until backup arrives.
- Once you have enough units on scene, form an entry party.
- Before entry into the structure, announce your presence as a law enforcement officer and issue commands for the subject to come into view. <u>Conduct no less than three announcements before entering.</u>

- Upon entering the structure, follow your department's training and practices to safely clear the structure.
- If a subject is found, secure, search, and identify them. Attempt to find out if there are more subjects in the building. DO NOT BRING THE SUBJECT WITH YOU AS YOU CONTINUE TO CLEAR THE BUILDING. Either have a unit escort the subject out, or leave two officers with the secured subject until the search is complete.
- If no subject is found and/or your search is complete, have dispatch attempt to contact a keyholder to come and secure the building.
- Have the point of forced entry processed for evidence (i.e., prints, photographs, etc.) and document everything you will need for your report.
- If a keyholder is unable to be contacted and the building cannot be secured, have dispatch contact your department's on-call service company to secure the building.

Chapter Two

ANIMAL CALLS

Animal Cruelty/Animal Abuse
Officer Safety Considerations:

- Secure the scene.
- Check if residents are home; this is to ensure you are not in their backyard and accidently perceived as a trespasser.
- Before making contact with the animal, check whether the animal is restrained or free. Often, abused and mistreated animals can be hyper aggressive as a defense mechanism to strangers.
- Don PPE, such as leather gloves/slice resistant gloves.
- Have a less lethal option readily available in case of an attack.
- Plan a route of retreat to avoid unnecessary escalation; we are there to help the animal not kill it if at all possible.

Objectives/Outcomes:

- Document the scene (i.e., take photographs of the conditions the animal is living in.)
- If the animal is abused to the point of near death (i.e., unable to stand, missing eyes or limbs, etc.), follow whatever policy directive your department has in place for euthanizing the animal humanly.
- If the animal is not immediately at risk of death, but there are potential aggravating factors that could lead to the animal's death (i.e., weather, lack of water, newborn puppies, etc.), then attempt to contact your local animal control to have the animal impounded.
- If the animal has evidence of abuse, but the officer does not believe the animal's life is in immediate peril, then document and report the incident. In this case, leave the animal there. In most states animals are viewed as property; barring an exigent circumstance, removal of the animal could constitute an illegal seizure.

Dead Animal

Officer Safety Considerations:

- Secure the scene.
- Don PPE (such as latex or nitrile gloves and facemask).
- If on the street, be sure to wear reflective vest.

Objectives/Outcomes:

- Notify your local city/county sanitation department via dispatch to remove the animal.
- If the animal is blocking a public street or accessway, remove it from the road or accessway, and then call the local sanitation department.

Stray Animal

Officer Safety Considerations:

- Secure the scene.
- Don PPE (such as leather gloves or latex gloves).
- Have a less lethal option readily available in case of an attack.
- Have collar or restraint device readily available to secure the animal once in custody.

Objectives/Outcomes:

- The primary objective is to contain the animal so that it no longer poses a threat to itself or the public.
- Once contained, and if the animal is friendly, you can check for a collar device and attempt to contact the owner.
- If unable to reach the owner, impound the animal and transport it to your local animal shelter.
- If the animal is contained but unable to be approached safely, contact animal control via dispatch to come and remove the animal.
- If the animal attacks, attempt to use less lethal force. If unsuccessful, apply deadly force to end the threat. Follow all of your department's policies in regard to using deadly force.

Chapter Three

AUTO THEFT CALLS

Stolen Vehicle/Victim Reporting
Officer Safety Considerations:

- Secure the scene.
- Check the immediate area for signs of the vehicle.

Objectives/Outcomes:

- Make sure the vehicle is a legitimate auto theft—check via dispatch that the vehicle has not been impounded. Additionally, while interviewing the victim, ensure that consent to use the vehicle has not previously been given (This fact is a defense to prosecution in many states and can often mean that there is no auto theft at the moment.).
- After the vehicle has been confirmed as a legitimate auto theft, fully identify the vehicle:
    i. Color
    ii. Make
    iii. Model

iv. Year
  v. VIN/License Plate Number
  vi. Damage
  vii. Stickers/Decals
- Good questions to ask during your interview include the following: Do you have the keys or are they with the vehicle? How many sets of keys do you have for the vehicle? When was the last time you saw the vehicle? When did you notice the vehicle missing?
- Have the victim write a statement.
- Give the victim their case number and your department's Auto Theft Unit's number to follow up on their case or report if the vehicle is returned or found.
- BOLO the vehicle via NCIC and your local network.

Recovered Stolen Vehicle

Officer Safety Considerations:

- Secure the scene.
- Preserve evidence.
- When handling the vehicle don latex/nitrile gloves.

Objectives/Outcomes:

- Confirm through dispatch that the vehicle is stolen.
- If confirmed stolen, have dispatch remove the vehicle from NCIC/your local database.
- If no one is in the vehicle at the time of recovery, photograph and get prints off the vehicle; impound the vehicle.
- If within your department's policy and if able to be completed within a reasonable amount of time, you can contact the owner of the vehicle and have them come out to the scene to retrieve their vehicle.
- If a subject is found with the vehicle, secure, search, and identify them. Investigate their involvement, and follow your department's training and policies to affect an arrest if required.
- Once processed, document the incident in accordance to your department's guidelines.

Chapter Four

BURGLARY CALLS

Burglary of a Business
Officer Safety Considerations:

- Secure the scene.
- Do not go by a civilian's word that the building is clear! Don't get complacent; clear the structure with at least one other officer, check cleaning closets, employee lounges etc. You never know who is still in there.
- Preserve evidence; don't let victim(s) touch anything until you process the scene.

Objectives/Outcomes:

- Once the structure is cleared, locate the area of entry, and try and walk through to see how the burglar maneuvered through the space.
- Take progressive pictures from the outside of the business, to where the burglar made entry, to

where items were stolen or destroyed, to where the burglar's estimated exit was.
- Process entry area and items for fingerprints. Good areas to check are: any glass surface such as door or shelve, countertops, and handles.
- Once the area is processed, interview the victim, determine when was the last time they saw the business secured, at what time did they discover the break in, what items were taken, and if they have security cameras.
- If the business has security cameras, ask to review the footage to get a good subject description.
- If the business does not have security cameras, check nearby businesses and residences to see if they have security cameras that may have caught what happened; detail those places in your report.
- Report and document all your findings. Submit evidence for processing.

Burglary of a Residence

Officer Safety Considerations:

- Secure the scene.
- Do not go by a civilian's word that the residence is clear! Don't get complacent; clear the structure with at least one other officer. Check closets, bathrooms, and under beds etc. You never know who is still in there.
- Preserve evidence; don't let victim(s) touch anything until you process the scene.

Objectives/Outcomes:

- Once the residence is cleared, locate the area of entry, try and walk through how the burglar maneuvered through the space.
- Take progressive pictures from the outside of the residence, to where the burglar made entry, to where items were stolen or destroyed, to where the burglar's estimated exit was.
- Process entry area and items for fingerprints. Check any glass surfaces such as doors or shelves, countertops, and handles.
- Once the area is processed, interview the victim, determine when was the last time they saw the residence secured, at what time did they discover the break in, what items were taken,

and if they have security cameras.
- If the residence has security cameras, ask to review the footage to get a good subject description.
- If the residence does not have security cameras, check nearby businesses and residences to see if they have security cameras that may have caught what happened; detail those places in your report.
- Additionally, talk to the immediate neighbors to see if they noticed anything around the time of the burglary.
- Report and document all of your findings; submit evidence for processing.

Burglary of a Vehicle

Officer Safety Considerations:

- Secure the scene.
- Preserve evidence; don't let the victim(s) touch anything until you process the scene.

Objectives/Outcomes:

- Take pictures of the vehicle to include the point of entry and the location of missing items.
- Process the vehicle for finger prints; good places to check are doors and windows.
- Once the vehicle is processed, interview the victim, determine when was the last time they saw the vehicle secured, at what time did they discover the break in, what items were taken, and if they saw or heard anything.
- Report and document all of your findings; submit evidence for processing.

Chapter Five

CRASH CALLS

Regular Crashes

Officer Safety Considerations:

- Properly place your emergency vehicle to provide protection for officers and the scene.
- Don PPE (reflective traffic vest).
- Request medical assistance for injured parties.
- Request additional support that may be necessary (Fire Dept., Crime Scene, etc.).
- Clear the crash off of the roadway as soon as possible.
    i. If it is not possible to clear the roadway in a reasonable period of time, you may need to manually direct traffic and/or place traffic cones/flares to divert traffic around the crash scene.

Objectives/Outcomes:

- Identify and interview drivers and occupants.
- Identify and interview witnesses, if any.
- Ensure all involved drivers exchange information; verify if the information is accurate.
- Determine if any traffic violation(s) or crime(s) have occurred and take appropriate enforcement action.
- Identify and protect items of apparent evidentiary value.
- Document the incident as necessary (e.g., collect insurance information, statements, measurements, photographs, evidence and reporting) on appropriate report forms.

High-Speed Roadway Crashes
Officer Safety Considerations:

- Properly place your emergency vehicle to provide protection for officers and the scene.
- Request Fire or EMS use their vehicles to assist in creating a barrier around the scene.
- Don PPE (reflective traffic vest).
- Request medical assistance for injured parties.
- Request additional support that may be necessary (Fire Dept., Crime Scene, etc.)
- Clear the crash off of the roadway as soon as possible.
    i. If it is not possible to clear the roadway in a reasonable period of time, you may need to manually direct traffic and/or place traffic cones/flares to divert traffic around the crash scene.

Objectives/Outcomes:

- Identify and interview drivers and occupants.
- Identify and interview witnesses, if any.
- Ensure all involved drivers exchange information; verify if the information is accurate.
- Determine if any traffic violation(s) or crime(s) have occurred, and take appropriate enforcement action.

- Identify and protect items of apparent evidentiary value.
- Document the incident as necessary (e.g., collect insurance information, statements, measurements, photographs, etc.) on appropriate report forms.

Aircraft/Train Crashes

Officer Safety Considerations:

- Properly place your emergency vehicle to provide protection for the officers and the scene.
- Request Fire or EMS to use their vehicles to assist in creating a barrier around the scene.
- Don PPE (reflective traffic vest).
- Request medical assistance for injured parties.
- Request additional support that may be necessary (Fire Dept, Crime Scene, etc.)
- Officers should treat an aircraft/train crash site as a crime scene until it is determined that such is not the case.
- If a military aircraft is involved, additional dangers, such as live ordnance or hazardous materials, may be present.

Objectives/Outcomes:

- Determine the nature and extent of the crash.
- Request additional personnel and other resources to respond as needed.
- Provide assistance to the injured parties until the arrival of EMS, FD, and/or other emergency personnel.
- Block off and contain the area to exclude unauthorized individuals as soon as practicable.

- Provide crowd control and other assistance until directed otherwise by a supervisor.
- Entering an aircraft or tampering with parts or debris is only advisable for the purpose of removing injured or trapped occupants, protecting the wreckage from further damage, or protecting the public from danger.
- Hold the scene until the investigative authority takes over control.

Hazardous Waste/Material Crashes

Officer Safety Considerations:

- Properly place your emergency vehicle to provide protection for the officers and the scene.
- Request Fire or EMS to use their vehicles to assist in creating a barrier around the scene.
- Don PPE (reflective traffic vest and hazardous material mask)
- Request medical assistance for injured parties.
- Request additional support that may be necessary (Fire Dept., Bomb Unit, etc.)
- Always remain uphill and upwind of the hazard zone until a safe zone and a decontamination area have been established.

Objectives/Outcomes:

- Attempt to identify the type of hazardous substance. Identification may be determined by placard, driver's manifest, or statements from the person transporting the material.
- Provide first aid, if it can be done safely and without the risk of contamination.
- Begin evacuation of the immediate area and the surrounding areas, depending on the substance. Voluntary evacuation should be considered;

however, depending on the substance, mandatory evacuation may be necessary.
- Hold the scene until trained units arrive and begin to process and secure the area.

Chapter Six

CRIMINAL TRESPASS CALLS

Criminal Trespass Consent Withdrawn
Officer Safety Concerns:

- Secure the scene.
- Frisk the subject on scene.
- Identify the subject on scene.

Objectives/Outcomes:

In cases where a subject enters with consent but fails to leave when told to do so by the owner or the controlling agent:
- An officer should observe the subject on the property.
- Have the owner/controlling agent ask the subject to leave in your presence.
- If the subject refuses to leave, make an arrest for criminal trespass.

- If the subject does leave, document the criminal trespass warning in a report. If the subject arrives back on property in the future, make an arrest for Criminal Trespass.

Criminal Trespass Notice Documented
Officer Safety Concerns:

- Secure the scene.
- Frisk the subject on scene.
- Identify the subject on scene.

Objectives/Outcomes:

- In most cases an officer can arrest a subject that has been given a previous Criminal Trespass Notice and is found on the property at a later time.
- Ensure the complainant is the sole owner/controlling agent and that the property the subject is on is not considered a public space or a common space.
- Check for previous Criminal Trespass notices for the subject in regard to the location.
- Criminal trespass can also be enforced if there are fences and/or signs in place obviously designed to restrict entry.
- Make the arrest, and report the incident in accordance with your department's guidelines.

Chapter Seven

DISTURBANCE CALLS

Business/Customer Disturbances

Officer Safety Concerns:

- Secure the scene.
- Establish police presence to deescalate any ongoing conflict.
- Frisk and identify the aggravating party; detain in handcuffs if necessary.
- Separate both parties physically and by line of sight.

Objectives/Outcomes:

- Identify the business owner/employee and get their side of the story.
- Interview the customer and get their side of the story.
- If applicable or necessary, interview any witnesses.

- Most cases are arguments over payment or refund; attempt to facilitate the process and find a resolution.
- If one is not easily found, do not force the exchange of money or services on either side—this is a civil matter. Instead, obtain helpful information for either side in the form of a corporate number, or advise they seek legal assistance.
- The business owner/employee may want to issue a Criminal Trespass Notice. If so, facilitate that process.
- Have customer leave the scene; document and report incident in accordance with your department's guidelines.

Family Disturbances

Officer Safety Considerations:

- Secure the scene.
- Establish police presence to deescalate any ongoing conflict.
- Frisk and identify the aggravating party; detain in handcuffs if necessary.
- Frisk immediate area for weapons.
- Separate both parties physically and by line of sight.
- Be aware that family disturbances often take place in people's own homes. Hence, weapons can be stashed anywhere.

Objectives/Outcomes:

- Identify and run all parties involved unless there is a clear primary complainant and/or you believe there is a potential victim of family violence. In that case do not run the victim.
- Interview all parties involved.
- Attempt to find a resolution to the immediate problem. Often, this is accomplished by having one subject leave the scene for a while to let things calm down. Remember if both subjects are residents and there is no crime, you have no legal ground to make a subject leave. You can only suggest so.

- If during the interview you discover a crime has taken place, take appropriate enforcement action.
- Afterwards, document and report the incident in accordance with your department's guidelines.

Disturbance Other

Officer Safety Considerations:

- Secure the scene.
- Establish police presence to deescalate any ongoing conflict.
- Frisk and identify the aggravating party; detain in handcuffs if necessary.
- Frisk immediate area for weapons.
- Separate all involved parties physically and by line of sight.
- Remember, these calls vary drastically and can encompass any number of variables, stay aware and keep your head on a swivel.

Objectives/Outcomes:

- Identify and run all parties involved unless there is a clear primary complainant and/or you believe there is a potential victim of a crime. In that case, do not run the victim.
- Interview all parties involved.
- Attempt to find a resolution to the immediate problem, this can look very different from one call to the next. It could range from roommates arguing over rent or eviction to road rage incidents to transients fighting in a transient camp. An important tip is that once the scene is secure, slow

everything down, find out what you are dealing with, and then execute your decision confidently.
- If during the interview you discover a crime has taken place, take appropriate enforcement action.
- Afterwards, document and report the incident in accordance with your department's guidelines.

Chapter Eight

DRUG CALLS

Drugs
Officer Safety Considerations:

- Secure the scene.
- Speed kills; you need to detain and secure the suspects quickly before they have a chance to run and/or ditch the evidence.
- Frisk all subjects for weapons.
- If drugs are in plain sight, conduct P.C search, if not than just frisk.
- Remember to check surrounding area for potential stash spots.
- Remember to always wear gloves when searching persons and/or vehicles for drugs or when handling drugs.

Objectives/Outcomes:

- Begin interviewing once all suspects are secure and there are no drugs in plain sight. Try to

establish P.C for a search, ask if there are any roaches, stems, or other paraphernalia in the vehicle. Admission to any of these will allow a P.C search of the suspects and vehicle.
- If you have no PC and no witness accounts and are unable to obtain any information during your interview, attempt a consent search.
- Conduct thorough searches on all subjects, ensuring you look in coin pockets on jeans, socks and shoes, inside cell phone cases, etc.
- Conduct a thorough and methodical search of the vehicle in accordance with your training. Keep in mind that the scene is secure and that there is no rush; don't miss anything.
- Upon finding a suspect illegal substance, take a picture of it in its original location and bag it in an evidence bag. Conduct a field preliminary test if needed/applicable.
- Take necessary enforcement action.
- Afterwards, document and report the incident in accordance with your department's guidelines.

Chapter Nine

FIRE CALLS

Building Fires
Officer Safety Considerations:

- Secure the scene.
- Call for Fire and EMS if they are not already en route.
- Clear out surrounding structures of people.
- Create a safety zone surrounding the structure.
- Remember that most law enforcement equipment is not fire resistant and will melt if exposed to high temperatures.

Objectives/Outcomes:

- Provide first aid to the injured until EMS arrives.
- If people are trapped, report the suspected location to the responding Fire Dept. Going into a burning building without proper training or equipment is not advised.
- Once Fire Dept. arrives on scene, they will be in charge; defer to what they request.
- Help secure perimeter.

Vehicle Fires

Officer Safety Considerations:

- Secure the scene.
- Call for Fire and EMS if they are not already en route.
- Clear out surrounding structures of people.
- Create a safety zone surrounding the structure.
- Remember most law enforcement equipment is not fire resistant and will melt if exposed to high temperatures.
- If the vehicle is a patrol unit, be aware that rounds will begin to cook off inside and create a hazardous situation for bystanders. Hence, create an appropriate safety zone.

Objectives/Outcomes:

- Provide first aid to the injured until EMS arrives.
- If someone is trapped inside attempt to remove them before the vehicle is consumed in flames. If not present already, suggest equipping your duty arsenal with a window punch device.
- Create a safety zone around vehicle.
- Attempt to extinguish or slow fire with a CO_2 extinguisher if available.
- Standby for Fire Dept.

Other Fires (Arson, Forest, etc.)
Officer Safety Considerations:

- Secure the scene.
- Call for Fire and EMS if not already en route.
- Clear out surrounding structures of people.
- Create a safety zone surrounding the area.
- Remember most law enforcement equipment is not fire resistant and will melt if exposed to high temperatures.

Objectives/Outcomes:

- Provide first aid to the injured until EMS arrives.
- If arson is suspected, treat the scene as a crime scene; attempt to preserve the evidence and the area as much as possible.
- If applicable, BOLO suspect description and any other important information to dispatch and responding units.
- Call in for additional resources.
- Check surrounding area for surveillance cameras that may have captured the incident.
- Afterwards, document and report the incident in accordance with your department's guidelines.

Chapter Ten

FLOODING/NATURAL DISASTER CALLS

Flooding Person in Flood Waters
Officer Safety Considerations:

- Secure the scene.
- Remember these situations are extremely dangerous and the risk of the rescuer becoming the victim themselves is a very real threat.
- Call for a specialized unit.
- Park your patrol unit out of potentially vulnerable areas in the event rising waters become more widespread.
- Wear a Personal Flotation Device (PFD) at all times during water rescue incidents. Discard most of your gear in case of accidental exposure to flood waters to increase survival chances.
- Keep personnel and citizens without PFDs a minimum of 15 feet away from the water's edge.

Objectives/Outcomes:

- Assess the situation, victim status, and water conditions and continually update dispatch.
- Only conduct a water rescue if the victim's life is in immediate peril or the situation is deteriorating rapidly and specialized assistance will likely not arrive in time.
- DO NOT SWIM TO THE VICTIM.
- Attempt to throw flotation aid to the victim.
- Report the victim's location to dispatch in case the victim is carried off to facilitate rescue effort by specialized personnel.
- Prevent bystanders from going in the flood waters.

Chapter Eleven

FORGERY/ID CRIME CALLS

Subject Not in Custody
Officer Safety Considerations:

- Secure the scene.
- Preserve evidence.

Objectives/Outcomes:

- Interview, identify, and document the complainant.
- Document suspect description and any other identifying information available. Review surveillance video if available.
- Secure evidence, including fraudulent checks, stolen credit cards, card skimmers, etc.
- Document and report incident in accordance with your department's policies and guidelines.
- Have victim make report to Secret Service if identity theft is involved.

Chapter Twelve

FOUND PROPERTY CALLS

Found Property

Officer Safety Considerations:

- Secure the scene.
- Wear PPE when handling foreign items.

Objectives/Outcomes:

- It is advised to only seize found property that falls under these guidelines:
    i. Are the items readily identifiable and traceable?
    ii. Are the items of value, such as money and jewelry?
    iii. Do the items appear to have been involved in a criminal offense?
    iv. Do the items constitute a hazard to public safety?
    v. Could the item be offensive to public morals or sensitivities?

- You should try to make a reasonable effort to return the property to the owner, when the owner is readily known.
- If the owner is not known and or cannot be reached in a reasonable amount of time, submit the items for safekeeping, in accordance with your department's policies and procedures.

Chapter Thirteen

HANG UP CALLS

911 Hang Ups
Officer Safety Considerations:

- Secure the scene.
- Park 2–3 houses/buildings down from your target location.
- Make a calculated approach; take in the scene, look and listen for any signs of distress or criminal activity.
- Survey the perimeter before making contact.

Objectives/Outcomes:

- Make contact with residence/building.
- Stay alert; look for signs of distress or criminal activity when contacting subjects. Look for any potential subtle clues that may indicate a need for further investigation (i.e., sweaty clothing, wide shifty eyes, or short cut responses).

- If you discover or develop reasonable suspicion that something is going on request entry into the structure or area to investigate. This should be completed with at least two Officers.
- If criminal activity is detected, take necessary enforcement action.
- If no criminal activity is detected, clear the scene and document in accordance with your department's policies and procedures.

Chapter Fourteen

MISSING PERSON CALLS

Missing Adult/Child

Officer Safety Considerations:

- Secure the scene.
- Establish police presence. Often family and friends may be emotional and need to be kept on track to further the interview process.

Objectives/Outcomes:

- Identify and interview the complainant to determine the circumstances surrounding the disappearance, along with the last person to have seen or been in contact with the missing individual.
- If believed or reported as a kidnapping, immediately BOLO the child's description information along with any information regarding the suspect over the air to dispatch.

- Ensure the person is missing, especially in the case of a missing child, by conducting a thorough search of the area where the individual was last seen.
- Document and identify a complete description of the missing individual, including name, date of birth, height, weight, clothing, hair, eyes, scars or tattoos.
- Attempt to secure a recent photo of the missing subject to submit for evidence.
- In the case of a missing child, confirm custody status and rights of the complainant. Additionally, rule out any possible involvement of the complainant in the disappearance of the child (i.e., kidnapping, interference with custody, etc.)
- Document and report incident. Submit missing subject's information for a BOLO into NCIC and your local outlet.

Chapter Fifteen

NOISE COMPLAINT CALLS

Loud Neighbor, Venue, Other
Officer Safety Considerations:

- Secure the scene.
- Listen, and survey the area. Always remember something more serious could be taking place.

Objectives/Outcomes:

- If original complainant does not want contact, and you arrive and do not hear an active noise complaint, it's best to not make contact with the residence/building and clear the scene.
- If the original complainant wants contact, but there is no active noise violation once you arrive, make contact and inform them that there isn't an active violation to enforce. List other routes of resolution such as civil filings.

- If there is an active noise violation in place, be cautious. Often house parties and social gatherings can leave an officer outnumbered, and alcohol can cause subjects to be hyper aggressive.
- Contact the residence. Do not enter; establish police presence and request to speak to the owner.
- Inform the owner of the active violation and have them bring the noise down into compliance.
- If a persistent nuisance, issue citations/ sanctions as appropriate for your department and location.

Chapter Sixteen

PARKING CALLS

Parking Violations

Officer Safety Considerations:

- Secure the scene.
- If in a vulnerable area, such as a high-speed roadway, don reflective vest.

Objectives/Outcomes:

- Determine if the vehicle is parked in violation of your area's ordinance or code.
- Determine if the vehicle is causing a hazard to drivers and or pedestrians in the area.
- If found to be in violation and/or a hazard, cite the vehicle in accordance with local area's ordinances or codes.
- Make a reasonable effort to locate the owner of the vehicle to have them move it.

- If the owner cannot be found in a reasonable amount of time, and the vehicle is creating a substantial hazard or inconvenience (i.e., blocking a resident's driveway), have the vehicle towed, if within your department's polices and guidelines.
- Document and report the incident as required.

Chapter Seventeen

PEDESTRIAN IN ROADWAY/ TRAFFIC HAZARD CALLS

Pedestrian in Street/High-Speed Roadway
Officer Safety Considerations:

- Secure the scene.
- Consider vehicle placement, especially on high-speed roadways, create a barrier and block traffic.
- Don PPE; often subjects in the street can be intoxicated and prone to violence.
- If subject is naked, wait for backup, follow at a distance, and update location via dispatch.

Objectives/Outcomes:

- If possible, stop traffic to avoid injury to the subject, civilians, and officers on scene.
- If the subject is not immediately recognized to be intoxicated, then detain, frisk, and identify.

- If the subject is acting bizarre, displaying signs of aggression to nearby vehicles or objects, naked, and/or screaming, be extremely cautious. The subject maybe in a state of excited delirium and highly resistant to pain.
- Create a plan, approach subject with at least four officers, be prepared to use force.
- Detain, frisk, and identify the subject once in custody.
- Open the roadway as soon as possible.
- For object hazards, such as cones, debris, etc., block lane of travel with patrol vehicle about 50–75 feet away from the object, don reflective vest, and remove object from roadway.
- If possible use tow patrol units on high-speed roadways, to protect the officers removing debris.

Chapter Eighteen

PUBLIC INTOXICATION CALLS

Public Intoxication
Officer Safety Considerations:

- Secure the scene.
- Don PPE before making contact with subject.
- Be aware that the subject may be in a heightened state of aggression; establish police presence quickly.

Objectives/Outcomes:

- Locate and make contact with the subject quickly; take note of the surroundings and what can be used as an impromptu weapon of opportunity.
- Frisk, detain, and identify the subject immediately.
- Call out for EMS.

- If the subject refuses EMS and/or is combative, effect an arrest in accordance with your department's state and local laws.
- Secure any evidence in relation to your case (i.e., alcoholic beverages, containers, etc.).
- Document and report the incident as necessary.

Chapter Nineteen

STRANDED MOTORIST CALLS

Assist Motorist

Officer Safety Considerations:

- Secure the scene.
- Be aware of vehicle placement to provide effective barrier against oncoming traffic, especially on a high-speed roadway.
- Don reflective vest.

Objectives/Outcomes:

- Before making contact with the vehicle and its occupants, run the vehicle through NCIC/your local network.
- Upon making contact, identify and run any occupants. You will potentially be in vulnerable positions while attempting to assist the motorist.

- Determine what is wrong with the vehicle and if it can be moved off the roadway by either escort or buddy bumper. Remember that the road is a dangerous place to conduct business; clear off it as soon as possible.
- If the vehicle's issue is minor, such as a flat tire, help replace it, if you have the knowledge and if it falls within your department's policy to do so.
- If not, or if the vehicle is beyond basic repair, call for a tow service to have the vehicle removed off the roadway.
- Document and report as required by your department.

Chapter Twenty

SUSPICIOUS CALLS

Suspicious Package

Officer Safety Considerations:

- Secure the scene.
- Approach cautiously and attempt to get as much information as possible before committing to touch the package.

Objectives/Outcomes:

- Make contact with original complainant. If at a residence, determine if the complainant or anyone residing with the complainant is expecting a package.
- Examine the package. If the package has a shipping label, attempt to track it via its package number.
- If legitimate, offer to open the package for the complainant, then secure the scene.

- If no mailing number or tracking number exists, attempt to google map the sender's address. If the location appears fictitious or suspect, treat the package as a potential bomb, and call for a specialized unit.
- If the package is reported in a public area, such as a restaurant, hotel, or bus/train station, use extreme caution. Examine the package/bag; always follow your instincts.
- Create a safety zone around the object relative to its size.
- Make contact with complainant, determine how long the package has been there, and attempt to view surveillance video of the area.
- Approach object, have radio and cellular devices secured, investigate the object as much as possible without touching or lifting it. Look for wires, and listen for ticking or mechanical noises.
- If seen or heard back out of the area and call for a specialized unit.
- Hold the perimeter.

Suspicious Person

Officer Safety Considerations:

- Secure the scene.
- Obtain a detailed description of the suspect.

Objectives/Outcomes:

- Approach cautiously as the nature of the suspect's actions are not known.
- Make contact with suspect, frisk, detain, and identify.
- Determine the suspect's intentions and motives for being in the area.
- If you develop P.C to believe a crime has or is actively taking place, take proper enforcement action.
- If no evidence of crime is present, have subject clear the area, and document contact as required by your department.

Suspicious Vehicles

Officer Safety Considerations:

- Secure the scene.
- Obtain a detailed description of the vehicle.

Objectives/Outcomes:

- Approach cautiously, as the nature of the vehicle and the suspects is not known.
- Make contact with the vehicle and run it through NCIC.
- If vehicle is occupied, frisk, detain, and identify the occupants.
- Determine the suspect's intentions and motives for being in the area.
- If you develop P.C to believe a crime has or is actively taking place, take proper enforcement action.
- If no evidence of crime is present, have subject clear the area, and document contact as required by your department.
- If vehicle is unoccupied but parked in violation of a law or ordinance, take proper enforcement action.
- If parked legally, but unoccupied, document and report the incident as required and clear the scene.

Chapter Twenty-One

THEFT CALLS

Subject in Custody
Officer Safety Considerations:

- Secure the scene.
- Make contact with subject in custody. Immediately frisk, detain, and identify.
- Do not ever take the Loss Prevention's word that the suspect is unarmed.

Objectives/Outcomes:

- Identify and interview the complainant and any witnesses.
- Make sure to review any surveillance video of the theft.
- Get an itemized receipt of the items that were stolen to use in your report and submit for evidence.
- Check to see if there are any enhancements for the offense.

- Take appropriate enforcement action based on the level of offense.
- Document and report the incident as required by your department.

Subject not in Custody

Officer Safety Considerations:

- Secure the scene.

Objectives/Outcomes:

- Make contact with complainant and witnesses; identify and interview.
- During interview, be sure to record time of theft, items taken, subject description, last known direction of travel.
- If the theft has occurred recently, BOLO subject description to other responding units.
- Make sure to review any surveillance video of the theft.
- Make sure to get an itemized receipt of the stolen items to submit for evidence.
- Document and report the incident as required by the department.

Chapter Twenty-Two

WELFARE CHECK CALLS

Check Welfare
Officer Safety Considerations:

- Secure the scene.
- Survey the area for signs of distress and/or criminal activity.

Objectives/Outcomes:

- If the check welfare call is regarding a neighbor or a family member that hasn't been seen or heard from for a period of time, attempt contact with last known residence and attempt to call last known number.
- If there is no response, attempt to see inside the residence. Look for signs of distress and/or criminal activity that will provide exigency to go inside of the building. If none are found, document and report the incident as required.

- If you do get a response, ensure the subject is fine and then clear the scene. If the subject needs assistance, contact EMS.
- If the check welfare call is regarding a potentially suicidal person, then attempt to contact last known residence and/or number.
- If contact is made, determine the subject's mental state and dispatch mental health services if needed.
- If contact is not made, document and report as required by your department.

VIOLENT CALLS

Chapter Twenty-Three

ABUSE CALLS

Child Abuse

Officer Safety Considerations:

- Secure the scene.
- Detain and frisk suspects.

Objectives/Outcomes:

- Quickly assess the situation and ensure the safety of all parties.
- Identify and interview all suspects, victims, witnesses, and complainants. Interviews should be conducted separately when possible. Do not discount the outcry of a child, often times they are able to report what is happening to them, even if they don't understand why.
- Determine the type and extent of abuse (physical, sexual, etc.).

- Take photographic evidence of the scene, injuries, weapons, or scars.
- Contact EMS if medical attention is needed.
- Contact a specialized unit if within your department's policy to do so.
- Contact CPS to open a case.
- Take appropriate enforcement action as required.
- If required or deemed necessary, remove the child from the household to ensure safety and well-being.
- Document and report incident as required by your department.

Elder Abuse

Officer Safety Considerations:

- Secure the scene.
- If the situation is dire, realize you may need to conduct a forced entry to preserve the life and well-being of the victim.
- Detain and frisk suspects.

Objectives/Outcomes:

- Quickly assess the situation, and ensure the immediate safety of all parties involved.
- Identify and interview all suspects, victims, witnesses, and complainants. Interviews should be conducted separately when possible.
- Preserve and process the crime scene. Take photographic evidence of any injuries, living conditions, etc.
- Assess and determine the nature and extent of the problem. Identify the type and severity of abuse.
- Contact specialized unit if required or available.
- Take enforcement action as required. Understand that arresting the abuser may take away the victim's primary or only caregiver. Arrange for the care and safety of the victim in this case.
- Document and report incident as required by your department.
- Contact and open a case with APS.

Chapter Twenty-Four

ASSAULT CALLS

Assault/Mutual Combat

Officer Safety Considerations:

- Secure the scene.
- Establish police presence; have bystanders get back.
- If the fight is still actively in progress, do not jump into altercation. Issue verbal commands to stop.
- If unheeded, use less lethal options, such as OC spray or Taser, to break up the fight.

Objectives/Outcomes:

- Once the fight is broken up, separate, detain, frisk, and identify all involved parties.
- Check for injuries, call for EMS if needed.
- Interview subjects and witnesses as necessary.
- Take proper enforcement action.

- Take photographic evidence of any injuries and/or weapons.
- Report and document incident as required by your department.

Assault/Aggravated Assault with a Victim
Officer Safety Considerations:

- Secure the scene.
- Establish police presence; have bystanders get back.
- If the assault is still actively taking place, use necessary force to end the assault and protect the victim.

Objectives/Outcomes:

- If on scene of an active assault, detain, frisk, and identify the suspect.
- Treat victim for injuries; call EMS if needed.
- Interview victim, witnesses, and suspect.
- Preserve and document any evidence. Ensure to take photographic evidence before EMS arrives to document the injuries. Secure and submit any weapons suspected to have been used in the assault as evidence.
- Take required enforcement action.
- If the suspect has fled the scene before you arrive, obtain detailed description of the suspect, including if the suspect is armed and the last known direction of flight. Relay information to dispatch and responding units. Afterwards, follow all the steps listed previously.
- Document and report incident as required by your department.

Chapter Twenty-Five

BOMB CALLS

Bomb Threats/Devices

Officer Safety Considerations:

- Secure the scene.
- Be mindful of radio transmissions and how that may set off the bomb.

Objectives/Outcomes:

- Locate, identify, and interview the owner of the premise, the person who received the threat, the person who has seen the suspected bomb, and anyone else who might know anything about the bomb/bomb threat.
- Evacuate the area and surrounding buildings. Establish a perimeter of 300 feet or more.
- Conduct a systematic search of the premise for potential bombs. The decision to search the premise should be made by the owner or controlling agent. You should also consider the validity of the

threat. If possible organize a team of volunteers, who know the layout of the premise.
- If no potential bomb is found, communicate the situation to dispatch and clear the scene.
- If a potential bomb is found, secure all forms of communication. Back out to the perimeter to communicate to dispatch and a supervisor. Document the exact location of the bomb, the time of discovery, and a detailed description of the device.
- Call for a specialized unit and hold the perimeter.
- Document and report the incident as required by your department.

Chapter Twenty-Six

DEATH/MURDER CALLS

Deceased Person

Officer Safety Considerations:

- Secure the scene.

Objectives/Outcomes:

- Don't touch anything, including weapons.
- EMS should be called in all suspected death cases, unless the death is obvious (decomposed, decapitation, etc.).
- Notify your supervisor.
- Gather information on the incident and the deceased. Gather name, DOB, social security number, any living relatives, attending physician, etc.
- Notify your proper specialty unit.
- If appropriate call for your crime scene unit.
- If the death appears to have occurred under suspicious circumstances, set a perimeter and log all personnel entering or leaving the scene.

- Document and process evidence. Take photographic evidence of where the body was found and in what condition.
- Arrange for body to be taken off scene once evidence has been gathered either by a medical examiner or a local funeral home. Stay on scene until body is removed.
- Report incident as required by your department.

Chapter Twenty-Seven

FAMILY VIOLENCE CALLS

Family Violence

Officer Safety Considerations:

- Secure the scene.
- Protect the victim of any potential family violence from further harm.
- Frisk the immediate area for weapons.

Objectives/Outcomes:

- Identify and separate the involved parties.
- Detain and frisk the suspected aggressor.
- If needed, call for EMS.
- Conduct interviews out of line of sight between the victim and suspect. Do not let the suspect talk to the victim by any means.
- If evidence of family violence exists, take proper enforcement action.

- Preserve and process the scene for evidence. Take photographic evidence of any injuries on the victim and the suspect as well as of the area in which the assault took place. Seize any weapons that were involved in the commission of the crime.
- If children reside at the residence, identify by name and DOB and contact CPS to open a case.
- Document and report incident as required by your department.

Chapter Twenty-Eight

HIT AND RUN CALLS

Leaving the Scene of an Accident
Officer Safety Considerations:

- Secure the scene.
- Follow the same safety precautions that would be required in a regular crash.
- Always wear PPE.

Objectives/Outcomes:

- Identify and interview the victim.
- If required, call for EMS.
- Interview and identify any witnesses. Determine the suspect driver's vehicle description, license plate number, and driver description. These details are extremely crucial for filing a leaving the scene crash; often a successful case cannot be filed without these critical details.

- Take photographic evidence of the scene, capturing the victim's vehicle damage, injuries, etc.
- Handle the rest of the scene as a regular crash, clear the roadway, tow vehicles as needed, and arrange transportation for the victim.
- Document and report the incident as required by your department.

Chapter Twenty-Nine

ROBBERY CALLS

Robbery – Business

Officer Safety Considerations:

- Secure the scene.
- If the subject was reported to be armed and in the area, have appropriate force option readily available.

Objectives/Outcomes:

- Make contact with complainant/victim. Identify the complainant and conduct preliminary interview. Obtain suspect information and descriptors as quickly as possible, BOLO information out to via dispatch.
- If needed, contact EMS to treat injuries.
- Secure the crime scene; do not let victims and/or witnesses touch anything before the evidence has been processed.

- Separate victims and witnesses and conduct detailed interviews.
- Contact your supervisor if needed/required.
- Review and document video surveillance evidence if available.
- Take photographic evidence of the scene and the victim, regardless of visual injury to the victim.
- Process the scene for latent prints if applicable.
- Document and report incident as required by your department.

Home Invasion

Officer Safety Considerations:

- Secure the scene.
- If the subject was reported to be armed and in the area, have appropriate force option readily available.

Objectives/Outcomes:

- Make contact with complainant/victim. Identify the complainant and conduct preliminary interview. Obtain suspect's information and descriptors as quickly as possible, BOLO information out to via dispatch.
- Clear the residence, ensuring no other subjects are still inside.
- If needed, contact EMS to treat injuries.
- Secure the crime scene, do not let victims and/or witnesses touch anything before the evidence has been processed.
- Conduct detailed interview with victim to determine what was taken and the possible motive for attack.
- Review and document video surveillance evidence if available.
- Take photographic evidence of the scene and the victim, regardless of visual injury to the victim.
- Process the scene for latent prints if applicable.

- Determine if residence is secure enough for victim to reside in, if not suggest alternative temporary arrangements.
- Document and report incident as required by your department.

Chapter Thirty

SEXUAL ASSAULT CALLS

Sexual Assault

Officer Safety Considerations:

- Secure the scene.

Objectives/Outcomes:

- Identify and interview the victim. Determine the nature of what took place. Did a sexual assault occur?
- BOLO suspect description (if the suspect in not caught).
- If the suspect is caught, take appropriate enforcement action.
- Secure and preserve crime scene. Remember there may be multiple locations, the victim, the suspect and the scene itself.
- Contact your department's CSI unit to process the evidence on scene.

- Contact your supervisor.
- Contact your department's specialized unit.
- If available/applicable start Victim Services for the victim.
- Take photographic evidence, regardless of visual injury or lack of a crime scene.
- Attempt to have victim agree to a SAFE/SANE.
- Document and report incident as required by your department.

Other great resources coming soon….
Police Officers' Guide: Texas Temporary Tags

Author's Ending Remarks

If you have found this book helpful, please leave a positive review on Amazon and help connect others to this great resource.

Made in the USA
Columbia, SC
23 October 2018